THE
CABIN CREW
GROUP INTERVIEW
MADE EASY

THE
CABIN CREW
GROUP INTERVIEW
MADE EASY

CAITLYN ROGERS

SPINEBOUND BOOKS

The Cabin Crew GROUP Interview Made Easy

Fifth Edition by Caitlyn Rogers,
Copyright © 2014 Caitlyn Rogers

Published by:
SpineBound Books
United Kingdom

ISBN: 978-1-908300-15-7

Printed in the United Kingdom
10 9 8 7 6 5 4 3 2 1

Library of Congress Cataloging-in-Publication Data
A CIP catalogue record for this book can be obtained from the
British Library

Cover Photography Credits

Photographer:	Andrey Yakovlev
Art Director:	Tat'yana Safronova
Style, Makeup:	Lili Aleeva
Hair Style:	Ovo Arakelyan

With special thanks to AeroFlot Airlines

SPINEBOUND BOOKS

www.SpineBound.co.uk

"Who said it could not be done? And what great victories has he to his credit which qualify him to judge others accurately?

- *Napoleon Hill* "

PART 1
THE INSIDE SCOOP

PART 2

SURVIVAL 101

PART 3

LIFTING THE LID ON THE GROUP INTERVIEW

Disclaimer
FROM THE PUBLISHER

This book is designed to provide information and guidance on attending a cabin crew assessment. It is sold with the understanding that the publisher and author are not engaged in rendering legal or other professional services. Such topics, as discussed herein are, for example, or illustrative purposes only. If expert assistance is required, the services of a competent professional should be sought where you can explore the unique aspects of your situation and can receive specific advice tailored to your circumstances.

It is not the purpose of this guide to reprint all the information that is otherwise available to candidates but instead to complement, amplify and supplement other texts. You are urged to read all the available material, learn as much as possible about the role and interview techniques and tailor the information to your individual needs.

Every effort has been made to make this guide as complete and accurate as possible. However, this guide contains information that is current only up to the printing date. Interview processes are frequently updated and are often subject to differing interpretations. Therefore, there are no absolutes and this text should be used only as a general guide and not as the ultimate source of information.

Get updates
ONLINE

Updates, special offers and newsletters will be made available at:

www.CabinCrew.guide

So be sure to stop by.

www.CabinCrew.Guide

Where dreams are made

My Dedication

TO YOU

This book is dedicated to all my readers who refuse to give up on their dream.

Thank you and good luck

THE
INSIDE SCOOP
PART 1

Contents
Of this Session

You can do it, if you believe you can

- *Napoleon Hill*

THE
TRUTH
ABOUT THE HIRING
PROCESS

The truth

ABOUT THE ~~HIRING~~ *elimination* PROCESS

We'd all like to think that recruitment personnel are giving their undivided attention to each resume they receive, and we'd also like to think that every candidate would receive a fair and equal opportunity to interview for the position. The unfortunate truth is, each airline receives thousands of applications every month. This not only puts a great deal of pressure on recruitment teams to reduce the load, but also makes it very difficult for any one candidate to stand out.

After seeing hundreds of hopefuls, it is only natural that faces and resumes begin to blur, with each sounding and looking much the same as the next.

> *"The process is designed to filter and eliminate"*

To address this overload, airlines have become highly selective and candidates are put through a gruelling screening process, whereby **hidden assessments** and **trick questions** provide recruitment personnel an opportunity to **secretly eliminate** large numbers of unsuspecting candidates as early as possible. In essence, the process is no longer one that is designed to screen for the right candidate or the best fit, but rather to filter and eliminate.

What was once a merely challenging process has morphed into a barrage of **trick questions, underhand tactics, psychological traps, and secret criteria.** Each designed to whittle down the numbers as quickly as possible, leaving those candidates who are unprepared and uninformed feeling bewildered and confused by the whole process.

It's not fair

While this process sounds unfair and brutal, it is not intended to be cruel or malicious. Rather, it has become an unavoidable means of conducting high volume and fast paced interviews within the majority of airlines. In order to understand the motives behind such recruitment processes, it helps to understand things from the airline and recruitment officer's perspective. So, let's consider the following statistics:

In 2012, Delta Air Lines received **22,000 applications for just 300 openings,** with applications arriving at a rate of 2 per minute. (Bloomberg: 2012) This is not an abnormal occurrence as Delta has also been quoted to receive **100,000 for 1,000 jobs** just 2 years earlier (ABC News, 2010). These statistics put each applicant at less than **2% chance of success.**

Meanwhile, Emirates Airline is "Swamped with cabin crew applications" (Gulf News, 2010).

"Applications arriving at a rate of 2 per minute"

Today Emirates are quoted to recieve over **15,000 applications each and every month**, with most recruitment drives attracting over 1,000 candidates. It is also recorded that, of the 400 candidates who turned up to a 2010 open day in Spain, **just 30 made it though** to the final interview. The Chief Commercial Officer of Emirates, Thierry Antinori, noted that **Emirates received over 129,000 applications** during 2013. (Trade Arabia, 2014)

Similarly, Al Baker of Qatar Airways reports "Qatar Airways was recruiting 250-300 cabin crew every month and that each open recruitment session saw around **800-2,500 candidates.** (Reuters, 2014)

As you can now appreciate, conducting recruitment drives on such a large scale is a tedious task for the personnel who oversee the process, not to mention an expensive one for the airline.

Hidden strategies
AND DECEPTIVE TACTICS

So, why donít airlines just recruit additional staff to handle the load?

All companies, not just airlines, are aware that candidates rarely show their true selves during a formal interview process. After all, it is only natural that candidates want to be seen in the best possible light. The problem is that some candidates will go so far as to put on a show in order to impress, and even mislead, the officers. These make it difficult for recruitment personnel to accurately gage whether a candidate truly is a good fit for the airline and its corporate culture, or is just playing the part for the interview.

Sadly, more recruitment personnel do not address this problem, so airlines have come up with an alternative strategy: A strategy that not only restores the power of control back to the airline, but also relieves the uncertainty.

"Airlines have come up with an alternative strategy"

Hidden surveillance
AND UNDERCOVER OPS

The fact is, additional recruiters have already been hired, however, these additional members of the team are not part of the identifiable personnel, but are part of the **undercover team**.

To help the recruitment officers make informed decisions and better elimination choices, undercover officers are often placed among the group during recruitment days. Within the guise of a fellow candidate, these officers can observe individuals in their relaxed and natural state, and be in a better position to extract information.

Information that would never otherwise be revealed is openly volunteered by unsuspecting candidates, as they are **lulled into a false sense of security and tricked into dialogue with deadly small talk.** Any mishap can land your resume in the rejection pile and you to the nearest exit.

These officers are largely accountable for the high percentage of failure rates that candidates experience during the group stage and are the reason why many candidates leave the interview feeling confused about their elimination. More significantly, it is those **friendly manipulation and underhand tactics** that enable officers to uncover information and eliminate candidates based on **secret criteria and other discriminations**.

"Information that would never otherwise be revealed is openly volunteered by unsuspecting candidates"

Secret criterion

AND DISCRIMINATIONS

It is no secret that airlines have stringent criteria for their cabin crew recruits. Among these, you will find minimum and maximum age, height and weight ranges, as well as health, fitness and grooming guidelines. These criteria are openly published and accessible to candidates through the airlines literature, however, **what candidates don't know, and what airlines will never reveal, are the secret criteria for which many elimination decisions are based.**

This secret criterion goes far beyond what is essential for the safe and effective conduct of the cabin crew duties, and even beyond what is considered ethical and moral. With no legal requirement to tell candidates why they were unsuccessful, most airlines have adopted a **zero feedback policy**. While this policy has been put in place due to the sheer volume of applicants, the protection this policy provides, sadly, leaves it **open to abuse.**

Every airline, from the largest international carriers to the smallest national operators, has its own **secret screening criteria**. As such, it is important to remember that, although it is illegal to discriminate, anything you share with the airline or their staff can be used against you without your knowledge. In such instances, these decisions can never be challenged or verified because such criterion are never openly discussed, nor are they written dawn. Essentially, they don't officially exist.

"Every airline has its own secret screening criteria"

Inconsistent
AND CONFUSING OUTCOMES

This lack of coherence and transparency naturally leads to very inconsistent outcomes for unsuspecting candidates, who may be viewed favourably by one officer, but not the next. Such exclusions appear to be without just cause, **leaving candidates confused and dejected** by the whole process.

"Unaware of the hidden processes that lie deep within the screeening process"

As the candidate struggles to establish a logical explanation for their dismissal, they tend to fall into a deadly cycle of overanalysing their own performance, often becoming overly self critical and then coming to the wrong conclusion entirely: A conclusion, which is often **taken out of context and to the extreme**. This leads to yet another problem, the problem of self-doubt and lack of confidence.

In the quest for answers, such candidates often seek out the comfort and guidance of others. Unfortunately, however, the guidance they receive is often from others who are just as confused as they are, as they too are unaware of the hidden processes that lie deep within the screening process. Sadly, this is also where the **myths and fear mongering** emerge, leaving the candidate feeling helpless and ready to give up on their dream.

The flaws

IN THE SYSTEM

For the most part, the motives behind employing these strategies are understandable. With the high costs incurred from the recruitment drives, not to mention the expense associated with the training and licensing of new hires, It goes without saying that **any mistakes made in the hiring process work out to be a very expensive and time consuming ordeal for the airline:** An ordeal that airlines will do anything to avoid.

"Under pressure to whittle down the numbers"

The unfortunate thing is that **it is often the innocent candidates who lose out** with such a system. This is because undercover officers are under such a great deal of pressure to whittle down the numbers, that **elimination decisions can be based on minor and negligible reasons.**

For instance, most candidates will experience some form of anxiety during an interview. While such a phenomenon is entirely natural and forgivable during the early stages of the process, the outward symptoms may cause a temporary shift in the candidate's personality. While this is not a accurate representation of their true character, the candidate may be eliminated before they have chance to compose themselves.

Unfortunately, this is a process that is unlikely to change as long as demand for cabin crew positions continue to increase. So rather than be discouraged by this flawed system, **it is time to take control** so that you can **work this system to your advantage.**

Work the system

TO YOUR ADVANTAGE

By understanding the process from the inside, **you can avoid being slaughtered by these underhand tactics.** You can tip the balance of power in your favour, so that you become the one who is doing the screening, not the airline. **No longer will you be cursed with generic run-of-the-mill answers and uninspiring resumes that have you looking and sounding like everyone else,** but will stand out as the top candidate that you truly are.

So whether you are a seasoned applicant who is finding yourself frustrated by another unsuccessful attempt or are a new candidate looking forward to your first interview, the **insider secrets and step by step guidance** within this book will give you a huge lead over the competition.

"No longer will you be cursed with generic answers and uninspiring resumes"

Discover

THE HIDDEN SECRETS

You will not find pages of information informing you about the duties, history and roster structures, and nor will you find average advice. **This book is raw and will take you behind the scenes to reveal secrets that airlines donít want you to know.**

The information is **universal**, revealing how candidates are screened and hired all across the world, from the largest international carriers to the smallest national operators. The information is **timeless**, so you will not find outdated or irrelevant advice, and, most importantly, it is **uncensored**. For the first time, you be shown how to avoid the common traps and pitfalls, and the true reasons why no airline will ever tell you why you were unsuccessful in your pursuit.

The hiring process is not always correct and it is often unfair, however, if you **understand the process from the inside**, you will never have to worry about what is expected or what recruiters really want to hear, You can enter the process informed and prepared, ready to come away with the job offer.

"Prepare yourself, for you are about to understand the screening process from an entirely different perspective."

WHAT TO
EXPECT

What to expect

The assessment process varies considerably in length and structure depending on a number of factors. These factors include: The volume of applicants, whether the sessions are held within the airline's premises or a hotel establishment, and whether the sessions are open or invitation only.

Open days typically attract a high volume of candidates and, as such, will often be split over a series of days. Invitation only days, on the other hand, are kept much smaller in number and may span only a few short hours with final interviews conducted on the same day.

In either case, you will be asked to partake is a number of activities. These activities are designed to reveal your personality, competencies and potential for working as cabin crew and are likely to include a series of individual assessments, practical tasks, group discussions and role-play scenarios.

Arrival at the event can seem overwhelming, especially when faced with hundreds of applicants in attendance. You will likely be met with an atmosphere that is friendly and buzzing with adrenaline, but has an eerie sense of tension, as each candidate is anxious to get through the process. This atmosphere generally tapers off as the sessions get underway.

Open day vs
INVITATION ONLY ASSESSMENT

When considering whether to attend an open day or apply for an invitation only session, there are two factors that will determine the best route for you. The first factor lies within the strength of your application, and the second is within your ability to stand out in a crowd.

Invitation only days rely on the pre-screening of applicants to determine suitability. If your resume appears weak, maybe there are large gaps in employment, or an apparent lack of customer service experience, you may be screened out before having an opportunity to explain such weaknesses. While it is possible to strengthen any resume, you may may prefer to bypass the pre-screening and attend an open day instead.

For candidates who struggle within very large groups, maybe due to a lack of assertiveness or a soft voice, the smaller turnout of an invitation only day may be a better match. Within these smaller sessions, it is easier to get involved, and even easier to be seen and heard.

In either case, the rest of this book will provide you with strategies you can use that will strengthen your application and your ability to stand out in a crowd.

A typical

SCHEDULE

In short, there is no typical schedule as to how many or which combination of activities are included during a cabin crew assessment day. Each airline has its own unique process and their schedules are updated regualarly.

In any case, you can expect that the group interview process will be divided into two key segments, these are: Group activities and individual assessments.

Group activities
During the group segment, you will be asked to take part in several activities. These activities are designed to reveal your personality, competencies and potential for working as cabin crew and are likely to include a series of practical tasks, group discussions and role plays.

Individual assessments
Individual assessments may be paper based, such as personality questionnaires and general knowledge tests, or they may be practical, such as self presentations, language proficiency and reach tests. Either way, these assessments form an integral part of the eligibility criteria.

A typical open day will be a two day event and might run as follows:

Day One
9:00   Arrive, welcome and introductory briefing
9:15   Airline presentation and icebreaker session
10:00 Resume handover
10:55 First eliminations
11:00 Preliminary group session
12:25 Second eliminations
12:30 Lunch break
1:00   Second group session
2:55   Third eliminations
3:00   Individual assessments and mini interview
4:25   Final eliminations
4:30   Debrief
5:00   Depart

Day Two	
9:00 5:00	Day two will typically be filled from 9:00 - 5:00 with blocks of panel interviews. These may be as short as 20 minutes in length, or as long as 2 hours.

A process
OF ELIMINATION

The primary objective during the group stages of the screening process is to filter and eliminate unsuitable candidates as quickly as possible. As such, it is normal to experience periodic elimination sessions throughout much of the day.

The initial eliminations will typically occur shortly after the resume dropoff, or first group session, but this is by no means absolute as schedules are changed regularly and without notice. In any case, it is this first elimination that is often the largest and it is not unusual for 50% or more to leave the process at this stage.

Naturally the elimination sessions are stressful, but if you make it through the first group round, you can be sure that you have made a positive impression. Now as you go forward to the next round, take comfort in knowing that it will be much easier to stand out with fewer numbers in the group, so build on the impression that you have already created and give it all you've got. Use the adrenaline from your early success to carry you through.

Just a number

Some airlines have negated to assigning candidates with numbers in place of using their names. This system of designation was introduced to streamline the process and to ensure that candidates are regularly shuffled. The idea behind the system is understandable and efficient, however, there is a disadvantage in that it leaves each candidate severely depersonalised. As such, you are no longer Kate, Alexander, Maria or (insert your name here), but instead you are number 284, 879 or 1029.

Such a system makes it all the more essential that you make an effort to stand out and be recognised.

When you only have

TWO MINUTES TO IMPRESS

During an open day, you may find that your first and only personal interaction with a recruiter will be during the resume handover session. During this session, each candidate will only be afforded 2 minutes each to hand over their resume and make a positive and memorable impression.

In many cases, the first eliminations will take place on this basis alone, so it is important that you make your time in the limelight as memorable as you possibly can.

Most importantly, remember to observe the officer's name and use it when you introduce yourself. Here is an example:

"Hello Judith, my name is Caitlyn and I appreciate the time you have taken to meet with me today."

While this may sound obvious, or even corney, you'd be surprised to discover how few will introduce themselves in such a pleasing manner. Those who take this initiative will stand out favourably.

THE TRICKS
THE TRAPS
AND THE UNDERHAND TACTICS

Your fate
AND THE *red pen*

Turning up to a cabin crew interview without a pen could spell disaster for your pursuit. Not only will you look unprepared, but the apparent lack of intention to take down any notes will give the impression that you are not serious.

For this reason, the recruiters will carry a supply of red, or green, pens so that they can easily identify such candidates when it comes time for processing the eliminations. Needless to say that any forms completed in red or green ink will be immediately rejected.

To avoid this very simple blunder, it is always best to carry two pens. This will provide you with a backup should one run out of ink or become lost, or you may need to help out a fellow candidate in their time of need. Just be sure that both pens contain either blue or black ink.

Colour-coded sticky notes

When it comes to feeding information back to the recruitment team, the receptionists use secret signals in the form of colour-coded sticky notes. If any red flags or doubts are raised about any candidate, a specific colour sticky note will be placed on their application form as a forewarning. If this happens, the candidate may be awarded a courtesy interview, but this is often as far as they will go.

Due to the nature of this trick, it is often reserved for the invitation only or final interview sessions.

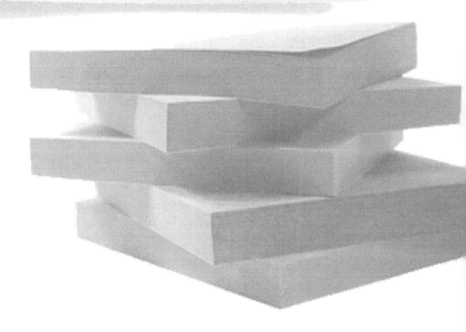

Secret spies

Whenever you are in the vicinity of the airline's territory, you will want to be watchful of your surroundings. Whether you are in the waiting area, at the front desk or in the restroom it is a good bet that employees, who have been enlisted to become internal spies for the recruitment team, are observing you.

The most obvious, yet often overlooked, internal spy is that of the humble receptionist. As the first and last point of contact, these powerful gatekeepers are in a prime position to observe candidates in all circumstances and from every angle. In putting on the friendly receptionist routine they are able to engage candidates in friendly dialogue, gathering information that can then be fed back to the recruitment team. Taking on a different approach, such as being rude or ignoring your presence, they will be able to entice and observe a different reaction entirely: A reaction that would otherwise not be accessible.

And what about the seemingly harmless cleaning staff in the restroom? Could they also be used for such purposes? Absolutely. In fact, It is within the so-called privacy of the restroom that candidates often vent their frustrations or bare their souls. So it is important to always be mindful of your interaction with anyone you come into contact with, even your fellow candidates. As we venture into the section entitled 'Undercover Ops', we will explore this aspect much further.

Caution:

SMOKERS

Due to the non-smoking environment on board an aircraft and the fact that you will not be able to step outside for a quickie mid-flight, many airlines now have a strict no smoking policy and will not hire smokers. So if you are partial to a cigarette or two, it is important that you refrain from 'sparking up' at any time before or during the interview, as the smell of smoke will linger on your clothing. Once the interview is over, you may of course have one, but be sure you are well away from the building.

To avoid your interview garments becoming infested by the smell of stale smoke, have your outfit cleaned thoroughly and then keep it zipped up in a suit bag away from your smoking environment. On the day of your interview, be sure to wash thoroughly before you handle it.

Although it is possible to try to conceal the smell of smoke, the effort required and the risks involved are far too great and it simply isn't worth it. The best course of action on the day of the interview is to wear a nicotine patch.

If you find the thought of not smoking for the day too much to bear, temporarily switch over to e-cigarettes, but be sure to use it only within the privacy of the W.C. and never in public view.

So, what should you say if you are asked whether you smoke? Well, this will depend on you. You can of course say no, you could be tactful with the truth and simply state that you have recently given up or you can respond in the affirmative. Whichever answer you choose is your decision, but beware that being honest in this instance may be the quickest way for your resume to hit the rejection pile.

In fact, you will find that many airlines now have this as part of the employment contract, so it is worthwhile considering kicking the addiction in the long term.

Avoid the traps

DURING THE ICEBREAKER SESSION

The recruitment personnel will often start the day with a short introductory briefing and a breakdown of the intended days events. This session should last no more than 30 minutes or so, and allows for any remaining candidates to arrive before the event officially gets underway.

The icebreaker session may involve a short presentation about the airline followed by an open discussion session. During this time, candidates are encouraged to pose questions to the personnel about the airline and the position.

This session is an ideal opportunity to get noticed early, but it can also be a breaking point for those who are unprepared.

Many of the more confident candidates make the mistake of getting carried away with their line of questioning in an attempt to stand out. Unfortunately, asking too many questions at this stage will only demonstrate a general lack of respect for others, who also have questions, and is also more likely to be misconstrued as arrogant, rather than confident. One question really is sufficient.

In asking questions, there is also the added risk looking ill prepared if a question appears unnecessary or has already been answered within the airline literature. This will highlight your lack of research and does not create a favourable first impression.

If you do not have a valid and effective question, it is better to just listen and observe. There will be many more opportunities to get noticed.

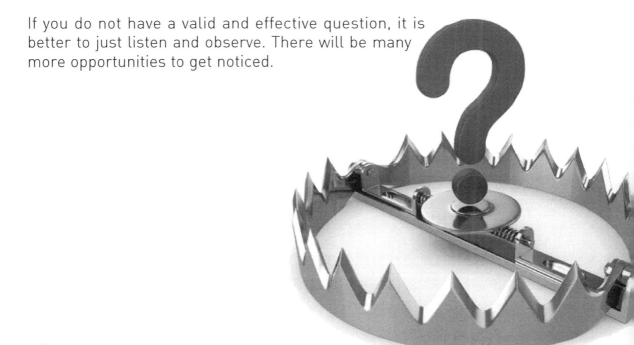

Complacency

AND THE WAITING GAME

With large turnouts, the group will often be split into smaller, more manageable sizes, and assessed in rotation. This means that you will likely find yourself waiting around for long periods between sessions. Although you will not be in a formal assessment during these waiting periods, undercover officers are still assessing you and it is important to remain professional and alert.

Too many candidates allow themselves to relax during these periods, and it is when they relax too much that they become complacent. Just take a look around next time you are at an event and you will see candidates slouching in their seat and generally looking very bored. Don't allow this to happen to you. Move around and network with the other candidates. This will show that you are taking the event seriously and are a friendly sort. As a side benefit, this will make time pass quicker and make the day much more enjoyable. And don't worry about what other candidates will think, as oftentimes they will appreciate your efforts to lighten the atmosphere.

Session breaks are a welcome relief from the mental and emotional stress that the day can induce, but these are especially risky times for becoming complacent, as many candidates do not realise that they are still being watched and assessed.

UNDERCOVER
OPERATIONS

Undercover

OPERATIONS

It is by no means a secret that candidates rarely show their true selves during a formal interview process. They will do their best to say all the right things, hide undesirable traits and say what they think the recruiters want to hear. After all, it is only natural that you'll want to be seen in the best possible light. The problem is, this makes it extremely difficult for personnel to accurately gage whether any one particular candidate is truly a good fit for the job, the airline and its corporate culture, or is just playing a very good part for the interview.

The task of filtering through hundreds or thousands of applicants is an arduous one and, to make matters worse, there are only a few short hours in which to accomplish it.

"Undercover officers pose the greatest threat to your success"

To relieve some of this pressure, undercover personnel are often placed among the group during recruitment days. It is these undercover officers who pose the greatest threat to your ultimate success, as their primary objective is to filter and eliminate candidates as quickly as possible, and for any reason they see fit. They are largely accountable for the high percentage of failure rates and are the reason why many candidates leave the interview feeling confused about their elimination.

Hidden
ASSESSMENTS

From the moment you step foot on the airline's territory, these officers are watching and judging your every move.

Your personal conduct, how you interact socially and professionally, and the information you reveal. are constantly being scrutinised and assessed. Any mishap or red flags raised during this crucial encounter can land your resume in the rejection pile and you to the nearest exit. There are no second chances.

Within the guise of a fellow candidate, these officers can observe individuals in their relaxed and natural state, and be in a better position to extract information. Unsuspecting candidates openly volunteer information that would never otherwise be revealed, as they are lulled into a false sense of security with seemingly harmless dialogue only to be enticed into mindless gossip and other undesirable behaviours.

During this critical period, officers are observing the reactions of candidates closely as they are encouraged to reciprocate and reveal all sorts of personal and private information. The observations made are then periodically fed back to the recruitment team, who are able to use the information to make informed decisions and better elimination choices in record speed.

It's not

WHAT YOU THINK

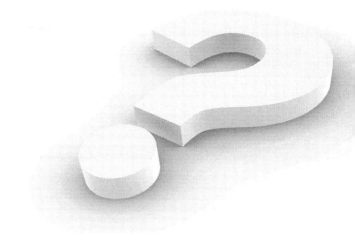

These officers are not interested in your level of education, previous successes, or best attributes; they are there to uncover information that could potentially cause problems or inconvenience for the airline. As such, the information gathered at this level is not necessarily sized up against the airline's corporate culture and assessment criteria, but rather the hidden criterion and person specification.

It is the information candidates reveal about their health, age, their likes and dislikes, and sensitive information about their background and personal life that are of interest to these officers. Likewise, they will be very interested to learn how you react to certain kinds of behaviours, people and pressures.

Needless to say, a candidate who displays undesirable behaviour or reveal questionable information will not proceed very far.

Shocking
REVELATIONS

It never seizes to amaze me how much information unsuspecting candidates will reveal when they think they are not being assessed. In many instances, it isn't even necessary to cajole candidates into confessing information, as many will openly share all sorts of things. Is it really any wonder airlines use undercover personnel?

Here are just some of the revelations I have encountered during my on site excursions.

Under the influence

"I'm so nervous I think I must have drunk a whole bottle of wine before I arrived."

Bunking off work

"I had to take a sickie at work just to attend this interview, so it better be worth it."

Admissions of deceit

"I had to lie on my application just to get invited to this interview"

Malicious Backbiting

"Did you see what that girl is wearing? What was she thinking?"
"That girl obviously has no brains. I bet she can't even read."

Negative intentions

"This is such a joke, I wanted to work for . . . but keep failing the damn interview so I have no choice but to apply for this one."
"I just want to work my way into first class so I can meet a rich, good looking guy"

The hangover

"I'm so hung over from last nights bash, I just want to go to sleep. Wake me when it's over."

Slandering the boss

"My stupid boss fired me, so I need this job desperately"

Many of these cases are rather extreme, I admit, however, they are by no means rare - I'm sure you've heard similar comments yourself.

As anyone can appreciate, it is these very mindless and irresponsible comments that undercover officers are seeking.

Innocent
CASUALTIES

Unfortunately, candidates don't need to be malicious or brash to be excluded from the process. A candidate who innocently mentions their looming personal challenges, such as going through a separation, in a custody battle, recently been made redundant, experiencing financial difficulties, or dealing with a close family member who is in poor health, could raise red flags as to their focus and stability. While such challenges are common and entirely understandable, such circumstances are simply deemed too risky for an airline.

What to expect?

While the above shock statements were made by actual caniddates, is it possible that such revelations could also be made by the undercover officers themselves as part of their mini assessment? Absolutely. It is precisely this kind of revelation that officers will use to entice a reaction or a reciprocal response. Be mindful, however, because such assessments aren't always this obvious or extreme. Assessments can be covert and very sneaky, so you always need to be on your guard.

Just as new cabin crew hires are put through an intensive training program, so too are undercover officers. These officers are trained in behavioural analysis and psychological profiling and, with this training, they are able to take on a variety of different roles and employ many different tactics. This makes them very effective at blending in and there is little chance that you will ever be able to identify them with any certainty.

The good news is that simply being aware of their presence and being prepared with a strategy will give you an advantage like no other. In fact, your informed knowledge and inability to be culled by their tricks and traps will make you stand out as a top candidate among the crowd.

Even better still, there is much more that you can do, not only to evade their traps, but also turn them into your greatest ally. All that is required is a conscientious and diligent approach.

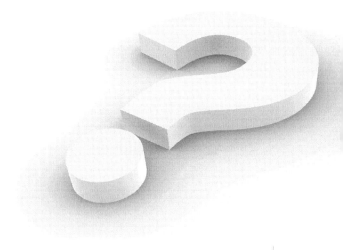

Your greatest ally

While it is accurate to say that the purpose of these undercover officers is to expose unsuitable candidates, they also have the power to approve candidates they deem to be exceptional.

If you are able to evade the tricks and traps laid out during this critical process and maintain a friendly, confident, and positive dialogue there will be no reason to pursue you further with trick questions. They will simply move on to another candidate when they are able to remove themselves from your presence. And if you are able to go one step further and create a connection with the officer, not only will you be put forward as a recommendation, but they will actually try to help you to succeed.

So how do you go about impressing these officers?

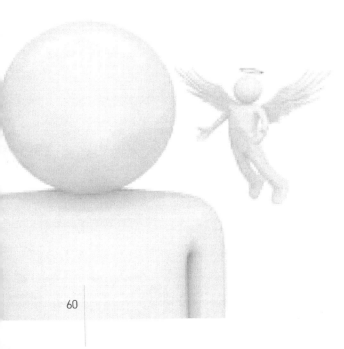

Create
THE RIGHT IMPRESSION

To impress undercover officers, you simply need to treat everyone you meet in the same positive manner. If you are friendly, respectful and supportive towards your fellow candidates, have a positive outlook and are able to demonstrate an enthusiastic attitude towards any activities that you are asked to undertake, the officers will naturally pick up on your positive energy.

Moreover, it is important to remember that anything you say, even in jest or small talk, can and will be used against you. Thus you should avoid volunteering inappropriate information, and your personal life should remain personal.

Naturally this can be easier said than done, so I have devised a line-up of potential scenarios to help you recognise and diffuse any situation you may encounter.

The Lineup

Undercover officers are like actors. They come in many shapes and sizes and their pseudo personalities are just as diverse. Because you'll never really know whether a candidate is truly a candidate or an undercover officer, it is important that you treat everyone the same. Here is the line-up of the common personalities that you may come across and how to deal with each of them in an appropriate manner.

 ## The Show-Off

You can be certain to find a show-off at every cabin crew interview. You will recognise him or her by their showy, self-absorbed and obnoxious attitude. While this personality type is easily annoying, the truth is that these individuals tend to be deeply insecure. They brag about their own achievements through fear that nobody will otherwise notice. Be kind and sincerely acknowledge their efforts when appropriate. This will demonstrate that you are not easily antagonised, but are also sensitive to the feelings of others.

 ## The Rival

In playing the part of the rival, the officer will demonstrate a very competitive streak, which puts you and everyone else as their competition and a threat to their success. They will attempt to make you feel inferior in order to throw you of guard. With these personality types, it is important to be friendly, but respectful of their space. Remember, competitive people are passionate, driven and innovative, so embrace these positive traits and don't let their feeling of superiority run you down.

The Show-Off

Gossipmongers like to point out other people's flaws or failures in an attempt to feel superior. This personality type is a favourite amongst officers because it can reveal a great deal about a candidate. Are you passive or assertive? Do you engage in gossip or show disapproval?

The best defence in this scenario is to first neutralise the negative comment by pointing out a positive and contrary opinion and then attempting to change the subject. If you have a tenacious officer, they may continue to press. In this instance, it would be wise to respectfully state that you would rather not discuss the merits of others, as it is not your place to do so. This honest approach should dissolve any further discussion on the subject. Failing that, it would be best to take your leave immediately.

The Think-They-Know-It-All

Know-it-all's have an attitude of superiority and like to think they are experts in everything. In conversation, they are arrogant and condescending and openly disregard the opinion of others. Remain cordial and patient and, whatever you do, don't be drawn into a debate, become critical or impatient. If the so called expert becomes overbearing or it is obvious that they are not an expert at all, you assertiveness skill s may be being tested, so you may tactfully and respectfully state the facts as you perceive them.

The Overly Anxious

The part of an anxious candidate is a prime opportunity to observe your patience and sensitivity. Experiencing a heightened level of anxiety is very traumatic and paralysing, so be friendly and supportive with these individuals. Offer words of encouragement, but don't place too much focus on their anxiety. Rather, try to break their state by asking questions about things they enjoy and that make them feel relaxed. You could ask them about their hobbies or desires.

The Negativist

Ah, the negativist. There's always one in every crowd and officers love to use this one to gauge a candidate's ability to remain positive under pressure. At best, negativists are very annoying. At worst, they will drain every ounce of energy and motivation from your body. If your attempts to motivate or encourage these people fall flat, remain positive and try to distance yourself as much as possible. If this is not possible, detach yourself from their words and stay focused on your own positive energy.

The Aggressor

Passive aggressors are covert and manipulative. They disguise their attacks as constructive criticism or harmless jokes so that, in the instance that they are confronted, they can deny any wrong doing. If you find yourself under attack from these predators, you may ask questions that will temp them into the open, such as: "Forgive me, but that sounded like a disrespectful comment, was it?" In the worst case, you may try to distance yourself.

If the aggressor is more openly disrespectful and disparaging, the best approach is to remain calm and composed, listen attentively and without interruption until they have finished. A counter attack will only reflect badly on you, so resist the tendency to fight back. Instead, acknowledge their opinion and then voice your own in a respectful manner or simply remove yourself from them as much as possible.

The Open Book

If an individual airs all their dirty laundry to you, revealing all sorts of personal hardships, it could be that they are looking for a reciprocal response. You may demonstrate empathy for their situation, but avoid getting drawn too deeply into conversation about of their hardship and avoid revealing any of your own. Changing the subject and pointing out the positive is always the best course of action.

The Unusual Suspects

The aforementioned scenarios are rather obvious, so they are generally easier to contend with. Where the traps really lie are in those personalities, which are not negative at all. In fact, it is the positive personalities, such as those in the following scenarios, which will often catch a candidate off guard. Because these personality types are friendly, approachable and easy to get on with, it is very easy to lose yourself in conversation with such individuals. It is with these personality types that you really need to be on your guard. So lets take a look at the contenders.

 ## The Extrovert

Extroverts are very sociable creatures and thrive on interaction. They are comfortable speaking to large audiences, are very open with their thoughts and feelings, and take an enthusiastic approach to most activities. This personality type is easy to get caught up in dialogue with, so you need to be extra cautious about the information you openly reveal when in their intoxicating presence. Enjoy the buzz they create and allow their enthusiasm to radiate through you and if you have an introverted tendency, just bide you time and make an effort to enjoy their vibrant presence.

 ## The Entertainer

Just like extroverts, entertainers are sociable, talkative and very energetic people. They love to be the centre of attention and often have an infectious personality. It is very easy to like the entertainer as they have a very down to earth and friendly attitude. When interacting with an entertainer, avoid being overly serious and just allow their positive energy to flow through you. An officer will use this type of personality to lure you into a false sense of security, so beware.

The Model

In using the term 'model', I am not referring to looks. Rather, I am referring to those candidates who seem to be models of perfection. They appear to say and do all the right things, seemingly without a care or worry in the world. They naturally exude charisma and confidence, and have a magnetic personality. Officers will use this personality type for two reasons. The first is so officers can gauge other candidates reactions to their presence, and two, they will be providing an example for others to learn from. In observing these candidates, examine what makes them appear perfect and be appreciative of those traits.

The Leader

Natural leaders are instantly recognisable by their innate desire to step up. Their confident, assertive and intelligent character inspires trust in others, while their sensitive, inspiring and sincere side inspires confidence. Officers will often use this approach to test a candidate's ability and willingness to support and encourage their fellow candidates without viewing them as competition. In the presence of a good leader, respect, support and encourage their efforts. Participate and be an active member of their team and you may just join them in the next round.

These are just some of the personality types that you may come across, but there may be many more. So always be on your guard with everyone you come in contact with.

Handling

QUESTIONS & DIALOGUE

Handling a personality type is one thing, but answering their intrusive questions or resisting deadly dialogue is quite another. So here are a few tips that will help you in this most critical part of the process.

Q: So, what do you do for a living?

This question is so common and seemingly innocent that it is easy to get caught out with. If you are between jobs, dislike your current job, or are desperate to find a new job this question can lead to and encourage negative dialogue. When answering this question, just remember to keep the discussion positive and be careful not to reveal too much about your personal circumstances if they are less than ideal.

Q: Don't you just hate interviews?

Let's be honest, unless you are like me and attend them for fun or research purposes, it is unlikely that you will relish attending interviews. However, just as you would attempt to diffuse a negative interview question with a positive response, you should do the same here. So, rather than admit to disliking interviews, you can state that you simply see it as a necessary part of the process in achieving the job that you desire and, therefore, you appreciate its necessity.

Q: This is my seventh attempt. How many interviews have you attended?

If an applicant asks you any questions regarding your previous interview attempts or current interview strategies you really must not divulge such information. You could attempt to change the subject in the first instance or, failing that, you may be polite and state that you would rather not focus on the past as you are trying to remain focused on the present.

Q: I had to take a sickie to attend this damn thing, how did you manage to take time off?

This question has many motives and your best response is a neutral one. Simply state that you have been preparing for this day for some time and have allocated time into your schedule for its purpose. There is no need to say any more.

Q: I want this job because ... What about you?

An honest and passionate response to this question will surely set you apart, so by all means share this passion if you feel it is appropriate to do so. Clearly the lure of travel is not appropriate, but you may be surprised that some individuals still use this line.

Q: My daughter decided to misbehave, today of all days. Do you have children?

This question is trying to elicit further information about your personal life. Rather than divulge this personal information you may choose to ignore it and just empathise by saying " Kids sure do pick their moments don't they? But you've got to love them". You may then attempt to change the subject. Asking follow-up questions will only encourage further dialogue and you will want to avoid this where possible.

Q: Why do we have to sing and dance? Surely this isn't part of our job description

This comment is trying to entice you to speak negatively about a task. This doesn't necessarily have to be about singing and dancing, it could be about any task. Even if you share their viewpoint, remain positive by indicating that you find such challenges fun and are eager to get involved. Nobody will know how you really feel if you don't share it.

Artful dodging

If you encounter a tenacious officer who continues to press your buttons or if you feel backed into a corner at any time, there may be no alternative but to relieve yourself from their presence as soon as possible.

In planning your escape, you will want to make it as seamless and natural as possible so that you can avoid, or at least minimise, causing offence. You could do this during a task or a session break when the individual is conversing with other candidates. This will make it less likely that your disappearance will be noticed. Whatever you do, be sure to have a plan in mind or you risk being left alone and looking like a lost puppy: This surely won't do you any favours.

Sure there will be a risk that a real candidate may feel insulted or upset if they catch on to your disappearing act, however, if your escape is truly justified, then such candidates are not worthy of your concern as they will only bring you down. On the other hand, an officer will at least recognise your ability to distance yourself from negative situations.

Now that you understand what you are up against, it is time to learn how to make yourself unforgettable...

SURVIVAL 101

PART 2

Contents
Of this Session

RESOLVE COMMON
CONCERNS

Resolve

COMMON CONCERNS

 Challenge: Perceived arrogance

Sometimes, a high level of confidence may be misconstrued as arrogance. If you feel you are sometimes wrongly labelled as arrogant, the following guidelines will help you maintain your confidence, while avoiding this assumption.

Be open
We all have weaknesses; to say otherwise will certainly make you appear arrogant. Be clear about what you do and don't know, and be prepared to listen and learn from others.

Be humble
Act with humility when you are recognised for a job well done. Acknowledge the effort of others by sharing and giving praise where appropriate, and be accountable when errors transpire.

Be approachable
To make yourself appear more approachable, use open and inviting body language, and adopt a warm, friendly expression. Inject some personality into your conversations, make good use of eye contact and remember to use people's names.

Be considerate
Genuinely acknowledge and compliment the hard work and efforts of others. Listen to and respect others opinions, and avoid interrupting when others are speaking.

Challenge: Being alienated

When there are a lot of different personalities in a group and the emotions are high, it can become difficult to get involved. This is especially true during a large group discussion. In these instances, you should employ some of the following strategies for getting your voice heard.

Raise your hand

As simple as it seems, raising your hand will demand the attention of the group and let them know that you have something to say.

Be assertive

If raising your hand reaps no results, you will have to be more assertive. Wait for a momentary pause in the conversation, and simple say, "excuse me" before proceeding. This may feel uncomfortable for some of you, but it is imperative that you contribute. If done calmly and respectfully, the assessors will be impressed by your effort.

 # Challenge: Being ridiculed

If your idea is ridiculed, resist the temptation to retaliate. Instead, remain cordial and respectful in your response. This graceful reaction will be duly noted and respected by the assessors.

Challenge: Handling disagreements

If you disagree with an approach being taken by the group or an idea, which has been brought forth, it is perfectly reasonable to say so as long as you are constructive and positive in doing so.

Consider the following statements:

Negative:
"That wouldn't work. I think we should..."

Constructive:
"I see your point, Mark, but there are a number of issues that may arise with that approach. How about we consider..."

The former example attacks and ridicules the idea, while the latter demonstrates a positive acknowledgement before a new idea is introduced.

In the instance that your new idea is rejected, remain polite and seek input from the group. If you are clearly outnumbered, gracefully accept the decision and move on.

Challenge: Feeling uncertain

You don't always have to give an opinion when you speak. Supporting what someone else has said, asking a legitimate question, or commenting on an emerging theme are equally good ways to make your presence known without appearing as if you like the sound of your own voice.

Points to Consider
In most cases, the outcome of each task or topic is largely irrelevant. Assessors are more concerned with how well you perform in a team environment, how you communicate your ideas and interact with others, and what role you typically assume.

Thus, no matter how you feel, you should approach every task with a can do attitude and every topic in a calm and conversational tone.

MANAGE YOUR
NERVES

Manage
YOUR NERVES

Nervous feelings before an interview are quite legitimate and most people can relate to feeling tense or fearful on the run up to such an event. In fact, a little interview anxiety can make you more alert and really enhance your performance, so you would never want to completely eliminate interview anxiety. However, when that anxiety becomes strong enough to negatively affect your clarity of thought and dialogue, some anxiety management techniques must be introduced.

Prepartion
AND PREVENTION

 Interview preparation

Anxiety can be the result of poor preparation. If you anticipate potential questions, prepare appropriate answers, research the airline and understand the requirements of the job, you will be better mentally prepared. If your mind is prepared, you will naturally feel calmer and more confident in yourself, and your ability to handle the interview.

 Remediation

Hypnotherapy, Cognitive Behavioural Therapy (CBT) and Neuro Linguistic Programming (NLP) sessions are very effective at dealing with deep-rooted anxiety issues.

 Medication

If you find your anxiety levels quite literally overwhelm you at interviews, you may be considering medication. While this is a method I don't personally advocate due to long-term side effects, there are over the counter supplements, such as Kalms, St John's Wort, and Bachs Rescue Remedy, which can really help take the edge off anxiety. Otherwise, your medical practitioner may prescribe stronger prescription medications such as Xanex or Beta Blockers.

Manage your mindset

Limiting beliefs are erroneous assumptions you hold about your own capabilities. They lurk in your subconscious mind and lead to self-sabotaging behaviours, which prevent you from achieving your desired goals. These beliefs are mostly acquired subconsciously through outside influences and, once accepted and imprinted into your subconscious mind, will dictate how well you perform, interact and grow.

To move forward, these limiting beliefs must be identified and challenged, and then replaced with more empowering beliefs.

Step 1: Identify

Clearly it would be impossible to challenge or change a belief that you are unaware of, so the first step to transformation involves identification.

Some limiting beliefs are obvious and can be easily identified by their all or nothing words, such as 'always' 'never', 'can't' or 'impossible'. For instance:

- My confidence always lets me down
- There's too much competition. I can't possibly compete
- The interviews are impossible
- I never say the right thing
- I always fail

Some beliefs, however, are so deeply ingrained within your subconscious that you may not even be aware of their existence. To expose these, you can use a brainstorming session.

Brainstorming is a simple, yet powerful, technique that produces raw material from the subconscious mind. To begin, simply sit down with a pad and pen, and start writing down everything that comes to mind about the interview.

If you struggle for a place to begin, you could use the opening line "I want to pass the cabin crew interview but..." then proceed to fill in the page until you run out of buts.

Asking relevant questions may also help, for instance:

- What meanings could I have created based on my past disappointments?
- What pessimistic thoughts reoccur every time I think about the interview?
- What unnecessary assumptions do I make about the interview?
- How might my standards be affecting my ability to relax?
- Am I holding onto any stereotypical beliefs that are holding me back?

Step 2: Challenge

Now that you have identified your limiting beliefs, the next step is to challenge them. By challenging your old beliefs, you create doubt. This doubt is all you need to be able to slot a new empowering belief in its place. Strong beliefs are not always easy to destroy. These can, however, be weakened when they are challenged.

Challenge the beliefs directly
The first way to break down a limiting belief is to question its validity. Challenge yourself to find evidence against it, and build a case that proves the assumption wrong. You could ask yourself questions, such as: How do I know this? Is it impossible or just hard? Is there another way I could look at this? Could there be another truth here?

Question the source

Do you know where your assumptions came from in the first place? Did you choose these beliefs or are they by-products of someone else's belief systems? Sometimes, realising a belief is not yours is enough to destroy it.

Challenge their usefulness

During your life, you have picked up beliefs that have not served you or were only valid for a certain period, but you have held onto them ever since. Ask yourself: Does this belief still serve a useful purpose? Does it help me move closer to my goals? Does this belief help or hurt me? If this belief limits me, how can I quickly get rid of it?

Weigh the consequences

The avoidance of pain is a great motivator, so realising the negative consequences of your beliefs may provide the motivation you need to destroy it. Ask yourself: What has this belief cost me in the past? If I don't change this belief now, what will the consequences be in the future?

Step 3: Replace

In this final step, you will identify and install alternative empowering beliefs. To do this, you simply need to reinforce each new belief with sufficient evidence to support it. Ask yourself: What have I done in my past that could contribute as evidence? What activities and actions could I take now that would strengthen this belief?

Keep a journal and continue creating evidence towards it. The more ingrained you can make the belief, the more evidence it will begin to identify for itself, and the deeper rooted the belief will become.

This step isn't an overnight process. It does take time to imprint the belief deeply enough into your subconscious that it will stick long term and overpower the old limiting belief but, with repetition and reinforcement, positive changes will begin to happen in your life.

Use your imagination

Since your brain knows no difference between real or imagined experiences, it is possible to use mental rehearsal and visualisation techniques to manipulate your physiology and improve your interview performance.

Find a quiet space where you're unlikely to be disturbed for 10-15 minutes and use these basic guidelines:

Get into a comfortable position and allow your body to relax. Take a few deep breaths and, as you exhale, imagine all of the tension slowly leaving your body.

Now imagine it is the day of your interview and begin to visualise the entire day, scene by scene, in your subconscious. When running through the events in your mind, imagine feeling relaxed, yet energised as you converse effortlessly with other candidates and the recruiters. Observe how others warm to your friendly and confident nature. Imagine your composure as you intelligently answer the interviewer's questions.

Make each scene as vivid and real as you can. Bring it closer, make the colours richer, sense the atmosphere in the room, and introduce sounds and feelings. Really intensify the experience.

When you are pleased with the imagined performance, begin to introduce challenging scenarios for different characters you may encounter, questions you may be asked, and pressure you may be put under.

Using this rehearsal technique for just twenty minutes a day will train your brain to actually perform the new skills and behaviours.

Repetition is the key to success with this technique. The more you practice, the better you will get and the more confident you will feel.

Anchor your state

Anchoring is an NLP (Neuro Linguistic Programming) term, which describes a process whereby certain psychological states, positive or negative, become associated with and can be triggered by a certain stimulus.

Using certain techniques, it is possible to anchor positive states so that you can readily access them on demand, or you can break the association of undesirable states using collapsing techniques.

Create an anchor

Step 1: Identify
To begin the process of creating an anchor, you first need to identify the desirable state. For instance: confidence, calmness, and assertiveness.

Step 2: Locate a memory
Next you need to recall a particular time in your life when you have felt the desired state. The context is unimportant, but the experience must have been a powerful one.

Step 3: Get into state
With an experience in mind, mentally put yourself back into that experience. Use all your senses to make the experience as vivid and intense as you can. What did you see? What could you hear? Where there any smells present? How did you look? How did you feel? Now really focus in and intensify those feelings.

Step 4: Anchor the state
When the desired state has been captured and the feeling is about to hit its peak, it is time to anchor those feelings. This is done by firing off a unique combination of cues.

The cue combination can include one which is visual, one auditory, and one kinaesthetic. For example, pinching the skin above your knuckles, while visualising the colour blue, and saying the word 'YES' is a unique cue combination that would be appropriate.

Step 5: Repeat
To really condition the anchor, repeat this procedure at least five times. The more repetitions, the stronger the anchor will be.

Step 6: Test
Now that your anchor has been installed, you need to test its effectiveness. To do this, you simply need to fire off your unique cue combination that you set up in step 4.

For best results, break state for a few moments and think of something completely unrelated.

If the anchor has been a success, the desired state should be experienced within 10-15 seconds. If the feeling is not satisfactory, further reinforcement repetitions may be carried out, or the power of anchor stacking may be introduced.

Collapse and anchor

Step 1: Identify
Before you begin the process of collapsing an anchor, you first need to identify the problem state (e.g. panic, anger, anxiety) and decide an alternative desired state that you would like to create in its place (e.g. confidence, calmness, assertiveness).

Step 2 : Create
Next you begin the process of creating anchors (See above). First you will create an anchor for the desirable state you want to capture and then you need to repeat the process for the undesirable state you want to collapse.

In creating the se two anchors, you want to create the desirable anchor according to the steps outlined previously, however, the undesirable state should be created with less intensity in order to give the positive state more power.

This can be done effectively by simply visualising the negative state in less context, using fewer senses, and only using one kinaesthetic cue (be sure this cue is different to the one selected for the positive anchor)

Step 3: Repeat
To really condition the anchors, repeat the procedure at least five times. The more repetitions, the stronger the anchor will be.

Step 4: Test
Now that your anchors have been installed, you need to test their effectiveness. To do this, you simply need to fire off your unique cue combinations.

For best results, break state for a few moments and think of something completely unrelated.

If the anchor has been a success, the state should be experienced within 10-15 seconds. If the feeling is not satisfactory, further reinforcement repetitions may be carried out, or the power of anchor stacking may be introduced.

Step 5: Collapse
Finally, you can begin the process of collapsing your problem anchor.

To do this, you simply fire both anchors at the same time. As you do this, your physiology will feel somewhat confused as it tries to achieve both states simultaneously. If the positive anchor has been created strong enough, the negative anchor will begin to clear. At this stage, you can let the negative anchor release, while you continue to fire and hold onto the positive state.

Step 6: Test
To test the success of the collapse, break state for a few moments and try to re-fire the negative anchor. The result should be neutral. If the state persists the procedure may be repeated, using the power of stacking positive anchors.

Ask resourceful questions

When you ask questions of yourself, you prompt your mind to search your internal memory archive for reasons and/or evidence to support those questions. So, whether you ask an empowering question, such as: "How can I achieve this?' or "Why am I so lucky?" or a disempowering question, such as: "Why does this always happen to me?" or "Why can't I ever get this right?" your brain will work to bring forth answers.

Wouldn't you rather have your brain bring back answers that create happiness and success? Well, why don't you make yourself a commitment to only ask empowering questions of yourself from this point forward? It's simple to do, and will really enhance the quality of your life.

Replace:
"What's the point? I never pass anyway"
"I always get nervous in interviews"
"Why can't I be confident?"

With:
"What steps can I take that will increase my chances of success?"
"What can I do to manage my emotions?"
"How can I feel confident right now?"

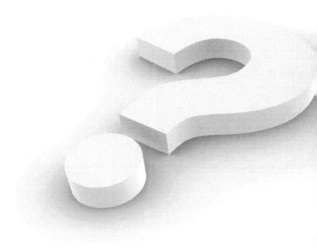

Create Compelling Reasons

There may be challenging periods that arise during your interview, which cause you to question your motives. If you have compelling reasons for wanting the job, your conviction will give you the driving force you need to carry you through these challenging moments.

So, ask yourself:
Why do I really want this job?
How will this job change my life?
How will I feel when I am successful?
What would I enjoy about the job?

 # Affirm & Incant

Affirmations are short positive statements, which are repeated several times in order to impress on your subconscious mind. To perform an affirmation, you simply take your chosen statement, for example "I am confident and successful in everything I do", and repeat it several times in quick succession with all the conviction and passion you can muster.

An incantation is a supercharged affirmation, which also engages your physiology. This action of getting your body involved creates a much more powerful outcome.

Depending on how deeply ingrained your beliefs are, you may experience some strong resistance as your brain attempts to challenge the positive messages it is receiving. Thus, the effectiveness of both techniques relies on repetition, conviction and passion. The stronger your concentration, the deeper your faith and the more feeling you inject, the stronger the results will be and the faster changes will begin to occur.

On-the-spot
RELIEF

 Deep breathing

Deep breathing will steady your rapid heartbeat, strengthen your shallow breathing, provide your brain with vital oxygen and make you more alert. Be sure to expand your stomach as you breath in, and not your chest. This will allow a much deeper breath to be taken and will allow your lungs to fill with oxygen.

 Change your focus

What you focus on has a direct impact on how you feel and what you experience. Therefore, anxiety is heightened the more you focus your energy on it. To gain some instant relief, you could try changing your focus. Instead of thinking about how you are feeling, how you look or what you are saying, re-focus your attention on outside sources. If you are engaged in dialogue you could listen more intently. Wherever you can redirect your focus will be much better than focusing on your internal dialogue.

Adjust your physiology

What you focus on has a direct impact on how you feel and what you experience. Therefore, anxiety is heightened the more you focus your energy on it. To gain some instant relief, you could try changing your focus. Instead of thinking about how you are feeling, how you look or what you are saying, re-focus your attention on outside sources. If you are engaged in dialogue you could listen more intently. Wherever you can redirect your focus will be much better than focusing on your internal dialogue.

BLOOPERS
BLUNDERS
AND FAUX PAS RECOVERY

It happens

TO THE BEST OF US

We've all experienced a blunder at some time or another, from the ill-fated slip of the tongue, to the embarrassing body blooper. You name it, it's happened to the best of us.

In everyday circumstances, bloopers, blunders and faux pas can be brushed off and, hopefully, forgotten. But what do you do and how can you recover if this happens during the all-important interview event? Do you laugh it off? Apologise? Pretend it never happened? Blame someone else? Make a sharp and speedy exit, or maybe a combination of the above?

Just in case the unexpected should happen to you on your big day, I have devised some stealth tactics and faux pas recovery tips. Hopefully you will never have to use them, but at least you'll have a strategy if you need one.

Three effective approaches

Depending on the severity of the blunder, there are three ideal approaches you can take: The first is to simply ignore it and move into a smooth recovery. The second is to hold yourself accountable and apologise, and the third is to simply laugh it off.

So let's take a look at each of these strategies further.

The smooth recovery

In many instances, you may choose to simply ignore it and move straight into a smooth recovery. This can be a great option if the blunder was mildly insignificant or barely noticeable. The risk with this strategy is that many will use it as a means to forge ahead and hopefully disguise their embarrassment. Unfortunately this urge to keep talking can make things worse if you are rattled or fixated on the blooper. Instead of making a smooth recovery, you may find yourself babbling.

After a blooper, it is natural to feel embarrassed, but it is important that you don't become fixated or concerned about the blunder or the recruiter. You'll stand a much better chance of recovery if you stop, take a breath, smile and continue on.

The artful apology

For moments that cannot just be ignored or brushed aside, there is the artful apology. Apologising for a blunder or faux pas is a great way to demonstrate a sense of respect and character. Rather than trying to hide or make excuses, drawing attention to the mistake and then apologising will demonstrate that you are honest and not afraid to take responsibility. This is an admirable quality and should not be underestimated.

Most people are willing to forgive, and you'll be amazed at how disarming a simple apology can be. Moreover, once a genuine apology has been made, the case is closed and everyone can move on from it.

It is important to keep your apology simple, yet sincere. A statement such as "I do apologise, my nerves got away from me there" or "I'm sorry, that came out wrong. May I rephrase that answer?" is all that is required. Once the apology has been made, shift the attention away and continue as if nothing happened. Don't give in to the urge to offer a lengthy apology, and don't bring the incident up again.

Be willing to laugh at yourself

When all else fails, having a laugh at your own expense may be the only way to disarm your audience and smooth over the faux pas. It will certainly lighten any awkwardness that has emerged in the atmosphere and most people appreciate someone who is willing to laugh at their own mistakes. If nothing else, it will show that are you aren't easily rattled and at least have a sense of humour. Not bad qualities I'm sure you'll agree.

It's how you handle it that counts

Whatever blunder you encounter, remember that everyone makes mistakes, and it is how you handle the mistake that will be observed and remembered. So whether it is the unexpected burst of flatulence, the skirt caught in the panties or a flubbed answer, if you are able to keep your cool and make a smooth recovery, the recruiter will appreciate your ability to remain composed in a challenging situation.

GROUP INTERVIEW

PART 3

Contents
Of this Session

HIDDEN
MEANINGS
BEHIND THE GROUP TASKS

What recruiters
ARE REALLY LOOKING FOR

This is the one question I am asked, time and time again. So many candidates overanalyse the process, but the answer is actually very simple. So simple in fact that most of you you will already know what I am going to say.

The recruiters are assessing six key competencies. These are:

- Communication skills
- Interpersonal ability
- Customer focus
- Team spirit
- Leadership
- Initiative

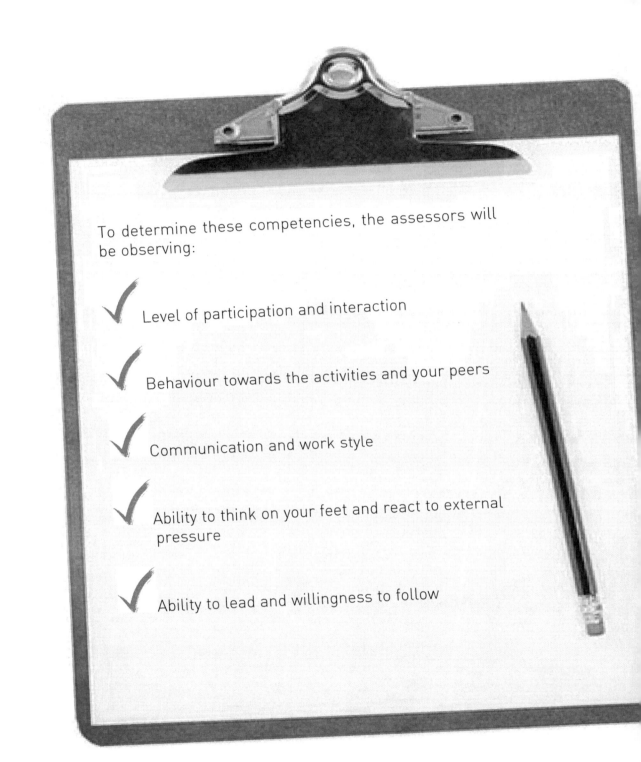

To determine these competencies, the assessors will be observing:

✓ Level of participation and interaction

✓ Behaviour towards the activities and your peers

✓ Communication and work style

✓ Ability to think on your feet and react to external pressure

✓ Ability to lead and willingness to follow

Where confusion

OFTEN OCCURS

Group tasks are designed so that assessors can view and assess these core competencies first hand, and how you behave during each task will be taken as a clear indication of how you may perform in reality. While it goes without saying that how you behave during an interview is not going to be an accurate representation when compared with a real life scenario, it is through your involvement and behaviour, that assessors can identify positive and negative attributes first hand and be able to make better elimination decisions.

Where most individuals often become confused is between the relevancy of the task and what is actually being observed. Because some of the tasks bear no obvious relevance to the cabin crew role, it is easy to overlook the underlying motives and get caught up in the practicalities of the task instead. And herein lies the trick: The outcome of the task itself is irrelevant.

Focusing

ON THE **WRONG!** ELEMENT

During this segment, most candidates are so intently focused on completing the task correctly and on time that they forget to think about their performance. In most cases, the outcome of the task is actually irrelevant. Assessors are more concerned with how well you perform under pressure and in a team environment, how you communicate your ideas, how you interact with others and what role you assume.

When you think back to the group tasks you have participated in, do you notice that they appear to have no right or wrong answer?

As an example, consider the following group topic:

Topic:

The plane has gone down over the Atlantic Ocean. There are eight survivors, but the one surviving life raft only has a capacity for four people. As a **team**, identify four survivors from the following list who you would save and state your reasons why. Select a spokes-person to **present** your decision and explain why you came up with the answer.

You (the flight attendant)   The pope
An ex army general   A surgeon
A pregnant lady   A child
An word class athlete   A nurse

Clearly there is no right answer to this topic, as you wouldn't want to decide such a fate for four people. So what is the point of this task? Take another look at the topic and notice the words I have emphasised are 'team' and 'present'. These are the keys to this task. Assessors are looking to observe how you interact as part of a team, and whether you demonstrate initiative and leadership by volunteering to present the information back to the rest of the group. Most candidates will focus on everything except for those two key points.

Let's take a look at another example: Singing.

Many candidates understand the concept of a discussion or role-play scenario, but just do not understand how singing bears any relevance. Again, this is very simple to comprehend if you read between the lines.

Task:

Many passengers ignore safety demonstrations because they feel they have heard it all before. In an effort to increase safety, Fly High Airlines is considering an overhaul of its safety procedures. As a **team**, come up with a new safety demonstration, which will encourage passengers to pay attention to these important briefings.

The demonstration can include appropriate humour, and must be sung according to the melody given to you on the back of the card. The outcome should be no more than **five minutes** in length and **each individual must participate**.

STAND OUT
AS AN INDIVIDUAL

Stand out

AS AN INDIVIDUAL

At some stage during the process, you may be asked to provide a self-introduction or introduce a fellow candidate to the group.

As well as learning more about you and your background, these self-introductions are an opportunity for the recruiters to assess how well you cope when addressing a group of people and how articulately you are able to communicate your message while under pressure. In their assessment, they will be looking for good delivery and a certain amount of charisma.

To deliver a presentation that makes an impact, the following page contains some guidelines for you to consider.

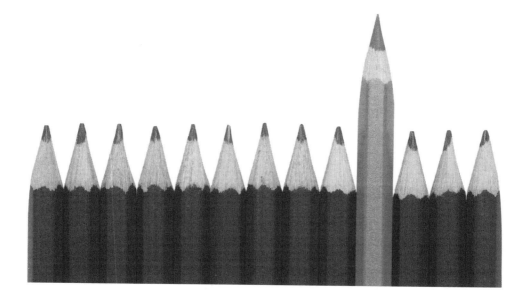

Make it relevant

Use this opportunity to highlight your suitability for the job of cabin crew by sharing interesting facts about your present or most recent job, and your motives for making a career change.

Be spontaneous

A self-presentation which is spontaneous, rather than rehearsed, will add life and sincerity to your speech. Sure you can prepare a rough draft and familiarise yourself with it, but don't try to learn it by heart, as there is a risk of appearing forced, dull and robotic.

Inject personality

Show your passion and enthusiasm by injecting some emotion and personality into your presentation.

Be concise

Unless advised otherwise, keep it relatively short and focused. Thirty to Sixty seconds should be sufficient.

Rotate your focus

To give the impression of confidence and engage your audience, rotate your gaze and make eye contact with various members for three to five seconds each, then be sure to redirect your focus back to the recruiters to finish your presentation.

Beware of how you sound

Varying your tone, pitch, volume and pace will eliminate the risk of appearing monotone and make it enjoyable for others to listen to. If you are nervous, you may be more inclined to rush. It will help if you make a deliberate attempt to slow your pace slightly.

Consider this example

" Hi everyone. My name is Caitlyn and it's really nice to meet you all. I'm 27 years old and live in the bustling city of Bristol. I currently work as a freelance hair consultant, which is a job I really enjoy, but I have always wanted to be cabin crew, which is why I am here today. Outside of work, I enjoy horse riding and am captain of the local netball team"

Seven
HEAVENLY VIRTUES

1 Have fun

However silly or irrelevant the tasks may seem, your active involvement is essential. So, rather than concern yourself about external details, just relax and allow yourself to enjoy the process. This positive viewpoint will reflect well on your character, demonstrate enthusiasm, and make the experience a fun filled one for you.

2 Contribute

Contributing ideas and making suggestions is another great way to demonstrate your enthusiasm and team spirit. It will show that you are able to express yourself and are keen to get involved.

3 Volunteer

There are times when no candidate wants to put their neck on the line, so volunteering is a great way to demonstrate your enthusiasm and it will show that you are not afraid to take the initiative.

4 Summarise

Summarising the main points of a discussion is a great way to move past awkward moments of silence and sticking points. The breathing room summarising creates will typically stimulate further ideas and encourage participation. Not only will your peers be grateful for the momentary relief, your communication and leadership ability will also be highlighted.

5 Use names

Remembering people's names will demonstrate your ability to listen and pay attention to detail. Moreover, it will demonstrate a tremendous amount of respect for others and create a lasting impact.

6 Be positive

When you choose to exhibit a positive spirit, people will naturally be drawn towards your character. So, be enthusiastic about the exercises you are asked to undertake and be encouraging towards others.

7 Encourage

If any members of your team remain reserved, encourage their involvement by asking if they have an idea, suggestion or opinion. This shows empathy, consideration and team spirit.

Seven

DEADLY SINS

1 Over involvement

Getting involved and showing enthusiasm in a task is fantastic, but over involvement and incessant talking can leave others struggling to get involved and may transfer across to assessors as arrogance. Always provide others with an opportunity to provide their opinion.

2 Under involvement

For assessors to make an informed assessment, active involvement from each individual is essential. Those who are unable to get involved, for whatever reason, will surely be eliminated.

3 Disputing

Conflicting views are natural, however, a group assessment is neither the time or place to engage in a hostile dispute with other candidates.

4 Criticising

Even if your intentions are honourable and the feedback is constructive, criticising another candidates opinions, actions and ideas may be perceived as an attack. An assessment day is neither the time nor the place.

5 Being negative

Making negative remarks or exhibiting frustration over tasks, peers or previous employers , no matter how harmless it may seem, will raise serious concerns about your attitude and ethics.

6 Being bossy

There is nothing wrong with striving for excellence, however, being dominant and imposing your ideas on others is overbearing and intimidating. This always leads others to feel incompetent.

7 Neglecting to listen

Neglecting to listen to instructions leads to misinterpretations and displays a general lack of enthusiasm. Not listening or talking over others is ignorant and disrespectful.

Active involvement

IS ESSENTIAL . . .

I know it goes without saying, and I've covered this briefly above, but it bears repeating that it is only through your active involvement that recruiters are able to assess your suitability and identify your positive attributes. So however silly or irrelevant the tasks may seem, or how difficult it is to get your opinion across, your involvement is essential.

Rather than concern yourself about external details, just relax and allow yourself to enjoy the process. This positive viewpoint will reflect well on your character, demonstrate enthusiasm, and make the experience a fun filled one for you.

I understand that it can be difficult to get involved when you are in a group of individuals who have big personalities. They set off on a tangent, leaving you feeling like you are on the outside struggling to get in. While these conditions do pose a difficult challenge, it is absolutely essential that you do what you can to be included. Raise your hand if you need to, but whatever you do, don't remain on the outside.

If you suffer from nervousness, understand that it is okay to be nervous, even permissible, but allowing your nerves to keep you from getting involved is not. It is better to risk displaying your nerves than it is to remain silent. At least the recruiters will appreciate your effort. If your nerves are strong to the point that you become debilitated, turn back to part 3 for in-depth guidance, tips and tricks.

. . . But

DON'T OVERDO IT

Getting involved and showing enthusiasm in a task is fantastic, but over involvement and incessant talking can leave others struggling to get involved and may transfer across to assessors as arrogance.

If you do notice that other members of your team remain reserved or appear to be struggling to get involved, encourage their involvement by asking if they have an idea, suggestion or opinion. This is a clear indication of empathy, consideration and team spirit and it is these qualities that recruiters will be impressed by.

Your scorecard

To make an effective evaluation, the recruiters will typically refer to a competency rating scale. This scale works on a points based system and the final result will reflect a candidate's suitability for the position.

-1 Unacceptable	0 Needs Improvement	1 Effective	2 Proficient	3 Outstanding

Score	Competency
3	Works effectively as a team member and builds strong relationships within it
0	Remains calm and confident, and responds logically and decisively in difficult situations
3	Understands other people's views and takes them into account
2	Contributes ideas and collaborates with the team
0	Takes a systematic approach to problem solving
3	Speaks with authority and confidence
3	Is thoughtful and tactful when dealing with people
-1	Is conscientious of completing tasks on time
3	Actively supports and encourages others
-1	Participates as an active and contributing member of the team

SAMPLE
TASKS

Bridging the Gap

Instructions

With the materials provided, design and construct a bridge which strong enough to support a roll of sticky tape.

Materials

- » 5 sheets of A4 paper
- » A pair of scissors
- » 1 Metre length of sticky tape
- » 4 Drinking straws
- » 1 Metre length of string
- » 2 Elastic bands

Let Me Entertain You Duration: 40 Minutes

Instructions

As you reach cruising altitude, you discover that the in flight entertainment system has failed.

To ensure the passengers are entertained for the duration of the four hour flight, design a game concept and present it to the rest of the group in a teaching style.

Advertising Space

Instructions

Fly High Airlines has secured a prime time radio spot and needs a new commercial campaign.

Using the team's collective <u>knowledge of the airline</u>, create a compelling commercial that will attract new customers.

The final broadcast must be no more than <u>45 seconds</u> in length, and <u>each team member must have an active role</u> in the final presentation.

Points to Consider

This activity will highlight your knowledge of the airline, so be ready with plenty of input from your research.

Designer Wear

Duration: 45 Minutes

Instructions

Fly High Airlines is looking to update its image and needs new designs for its cabin crew uniform.

Consider the existing design and come up with a new or modified concept.

Points to Consider

During this task, be mindful of what is considered appropriate to the culture.

Also, take inspiration from the current design as it provides valuable insight into what the airline considers to be appropriate.

GROUP
DISCUSSIONS

Survivor

Instructions

Your flight is scheduled to land in Los Angeles, however, due to mechanical difficulties the plane was forced to land on a remote island.

During landing, much of the equipment aboard was damaged, but 10 items have been recovered intact. Your task is to rank them in terms of their importance for your crew.

Items

- » A box of matches
- » 15 feet of nylon rope
- » 5 gallons of water
- » Signal flares
- » A self inflating life raft
- » A magnetic compass
- » First aid kit
- » A fruit basket
- » A tub of dry milk powder
- » A shotgun

Day Trip

Duration: 30 Minutes

Instructions

You have been given the responsibility for arranging a day trip for 15 disabled children. Discuss where you would take the children, what activities you would have arranged and why.

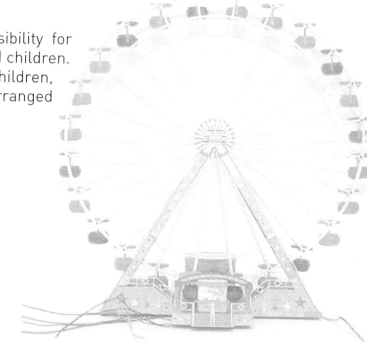

Options

» Theme park

» Museum

» White water rafting

» Trip on the Orient Express

» Water Park

» Safari

» Art gallery

» Scenic helicopter ride

Points to Consider

In this instance, the children in question are disabled. So, certain activities will not be appropriate, while others may not sufficiently capture the children's interest. It is important to gain a balance between having fun and being safe.

ROLE PLAY
SCENARIOS

Role-play

SCENARIOS

Role-play scenarios may be performed with other candidates as a pair or within a group, or they may be performed one on one with an assessor.

The scenarios will bear some relation to the demands of the job and are likely to include:

Intoxicated passenger	Disorderly behaviour
Terrorist threat	Disruptive child
Toilet smoker	Abusive behaviour
Fearful passenger	Passenger complaint

The assessors don't expect you to know the answer to every possible scenario they introduce. They simply want to see how you react in challenging situations. So, when taking part in any role play scenario, use the following guidelines:

• Be proactive and do your best to resolve the situation using your initiative
• Remain calm and composed
• Be direct and assertive
• Immerse yourself into the role
• Take each scenario seriously
• Devise a plan and follow it as much as possible

Here are some pointers to help you deal with some common scenarios:

Complaint

In the case of a passenger complaint, it is important that you listen to their concern without interruption. Ask questions, where appropriate, to clarify their concerns and show empathy towards their situation. If the facts warrant it, apologise for the situation, explain what action you intend to take and thank them for bringing the matter to your attention.

Fearful passenger

If a passenger is fearful of flying, be considerate of their feelings. Use a gentle and calm tone to talk them through the flight and reassure them of any sounds or sensations they may experience. Let the passenger know where you can be found and show them the call bell.

Intoxicated passenger

Offer the passenger a cup of tea or coffee and don't provide any more alcoholic drinks. You could also encourage the passenger to eat some food. Remain calm towards the passenger, but be direct and assertive in your approach. If you feel it appropriate, inform your senior and seek assistance from other crewmembers.

The group tasks and discussion are updated regularly, so the above examples are only for demonstration purposes. In any case, remember that the outcome of the task is irrelevant. Always be mindful of your behaviour and how you are being percieved by those around you.

THE
TESTING STAGE

Important tips
AND ADVICE

When carrying out any kind of test, it is important that you read the questions through fully and make sure you completely understand what is being asked before attempting to answer. Nothing looks more sloppy or unprepared than handing in a test sheet with scribbles and corrections all over it.

Begin by going through the test sheet and completing all the questions you find easy. With this strategy, you can be confident that you have at least answered as many questions as possible should you get stuck on other trickier questions for an extended period of time.

It is also a good idea to go through a final check when you are finished to ensure that no mistakes have been made inadvertently. If you have sufficient time, you may mark your answers in pencil first, so that when you are completing your final check any mistakes can be easily rectified.

Psychometric

AND PERSONALITY PROFILE

It is believed that psychometric tests provide a clear assessment of a candidate's ability to carry out a job, and whether the character of an individual will complement the current working environment.

Psychometric testing helps to build a profile of characteristics, behavioural style and personality. For example, how does a candidate interact with others? How do they react within a certain situation? Is a candidate able to do the job for which they have applied? Is a candidate a natural leader with individual initiative? Etc...

The reason airlines use psychometric testing during the recruitment process is because they have a clear idea of the sort of person they are looking to recruit. If you are not the sort of person the airline are looking for, then you are unlikely to be happy in the job in the long term, no matter how superficially attractive it may be.

Trying to beat the system

When approaching a psychometric test, it is important to answer the questions as honestly as possible. It is understandable that you will want to create a favourable impression, and you may even be tempted to tailor your answers according to what you think the airline want to hear, but falsifying your answers will only lead to unnatural and inconsistent results.

Moreover, the correct answer may not always be obvious, as they are often written in a way that makes it difficult to distinguish. Take the following question for instance: 'I prefer to work independently, rather than in a team'.

On first impressions, disagreeing with this answer may seem like the obvious choice, after all teamwork is an important aspect of the cabin crew role, right? However, if you think about the question from an alternative perspective, it may be that the airline is trying to ascertain if you are able and willing to use your own initiative, another important quality. So, what about a middle of the road answer? One or two middle of the road answers are acceptable, however, too many will make you appear indecisive and unsure, and you many not reach the minimum required score. So what is the best answer? It's simple, the best answer is the one that is honest.

A decision-making tool

The psychometric test is no doubt a valuable assessment tool, however, it is not an instant pass or fail decision-making tool. It is used simply as a supplement what the assessors have already observed about you and your involvement during the assessment day. If you answered the above example in the affirmative, and you also demonstrated the ability to work well within a team environment, both aspects will be taken into consideration.

An example

The tests you are given will be updated often, however, here is a basic example of how a psychometric assessment is generally carried out and the types of questions you can expect to be asked...

Mark each of the following statements on a scale of 1 to 5 where:
1 = Strongly agree   2 = Agree   3 = Not sure   4 = Disagree   5 = Strongly disagree

1	At work, I like to be told exactly what to do	1	2	3	4	5
2	If you want something done properly, you have to do it yourself	1	2	3	4	5
3	We often need help and advice from our superiors	1	2	3	4	5
4	I find it easy to relax after a hard day	1	2	3	4	5
5	I would like to win the lottery and retire early	1	2	3	4	5
6	Most people are honest	1	2	3	4	5
7	I have a career development plan in mind	1	2	3	4	5
8	I believe that the end justifies the means	1	2	3	4	5
9	Would you prefer to be an author (1) or an actor (2)	1	2	?		
10	I can achieve anything if I try hard enough	1	2	3	4	5
11	I enjoy meeting new people	1	2	3	4	5
12	I get bored doing repetitive tasks	1	2	3	4	5
13	I often lose my temper when I am frustrated	1	2	3	4	5
14	Who do you admire more – Madonna (1) or Mahatma Gandhi (2)	1	2	?		
15	I need alcohol to give me confidence around other people	1	2	3	4	5
16	I prefer working independently rather than in a team	1	2	3	4	5
17	I fall sick often	1	2	3	4	5
18	I always think before I act	1	2	3	4	5
19	I respect my superiors decisions even if I don't agree	1	2	3	4	5
20	I knew what career I wanted when I left school	1	2	3	4	5
21	Worrying keeps me awake at night	1	2	3	4	5
22	I am often lost for words when meeting people for the first time	1	2	3	4	5
23	I feel dissatisfied with my career progress to date	1	2	3	4	5
24	Are you more introvert (1) or extrovert (2)	1	2	?		
25	I often feel overwhelmed	1	2	3	4	5
26	I enjoy challenges	1	2	3	4	5
27	I make mistakes when I rush	1	2	3	4	5
28	I have an active social life	1	2	3	4	5
29	I sometimes feel depressed with my life	1	2	3	4	5
30	Do you prefer using the stairs (1) or an escalator (2)	1	2	?		

31	I feel confident about my future	1	2	3	4	5
32	I plan activities rather than just going ahead and doing it	1	2	3	4	5
33	I can't work with people I don't like	1	2	3	4	5
34	I listen politely to people with whom I deeply disagree	1	2	3	4	5
35	I find it difficult to bounce back after disappointment	1	2	3	4	5
36	Do you prefer to work with your hands (1) or your brain (2)	1	2	?		
37	I value my reputation for straight talking	1	2	3	4	5
38	When I worry, I bottle it up inside	1	2	3	4	5
39	I need others to motivate me	1	2	3	4	5
40	I can work on my own initiative	1	2	3	4	5
41	I am easily stressed	1	2	3	4	5
42	Are you more productive in the morning (1) or in the evening (2)	1	2	?		
43	I would make a good salesperson	1	2	3	4	5
44	I tire easily	1	2	3	4	5
45	I stand up for what I believe	1	2	3	4	5
46	I sometimes cut corners to get a job done quicker	1	2	3	4	5
47	I would like to be somebody else	1	2	3	4	5
48	Would you rather sit and read a book (1) or go for a walk (2)	1	2	?		
49	I sometimes lie to get what I want	1	2	3	4	5
50	I am a good leader	1	2	3	4	5
51	I take criticism personally	1	2	3	4	5
52	I am a fast learner	1	2	3	4	5
53	Is it more important to be truthful (1) or tactful (2)	1	2	?		
54	I feel most relaxed in my own company	1	2	3	4	5
55	Do you prefer to talk (1) or listen (2)	1	2	?		
56	I remain calm under pressure	1	2	3	4	5
57	I am often late arriving at work	1	2	3	4	5
58	People respect my opinions	1	2	3	4	5
59	I would leave work immediately if a family member became ill	1	2	3	4	5
60	I am confident when addressing a group	1	2	3	4	5

English
COMPREHENSION

The ability to speak and comprehend English is essential for the role of cabin crew and your English proficiency will be observed and evaluated throughout the course of the assessment. If English isn't your native language, you will also be required to pass an English comprehension assessment.

The 'Test of English as a Foreign Language' (TOEFL) system is used for this purpose, and I recommend seeking further study in this area if you have concerns in your ability. There are several books I recommend for this purpose, and these are noted within the Bibliography section at the back of the book.

For the English comprehension test, you can expect to be assessed on the following four areas:

- Listening
- Reading
- Writing
- Speaking

These skills can be assessed within three modes of communication:

· Interpersonal (involving two-way interactive communication)
· Interpretive (relating to the understanding of spoken or written language)
· Presentational (involving creating spoken or written communication)

Performance on assessment tasks will be evaluated by how well you understand (comprehension) and can be understood (comprehensibility). The evaluation considers language knowledge, the appropriate use of communication strategies, and the application of cultural knowledge to enhance communication.

THE
CONCLUSION
WHAT NEXT?

Coping with

SETBACKS

It may seem counter intuitive to provide coping strategies for rejection in an interview guidance book, however, in an industry such as this, where supply exceeds demand, rejection is an unfortunate outcome that some candidates will ultimately face.

So, rather than be crushed by this outcome, I have put together the following tips for coping with, learning from and moving forward following a setback.

Prepare

The popular saying 'Prepare for the worst, but hope for the best' certainly applies in interview scenarios. If you attend the interview with an open mind, your attitude will be more relaxed, you will be better prepared and your coping abilities will be greatly enhanced.

Assess

Faced with rejection, it can be easy to misplace blame on yourself, others or on the general circumstances. But, if you are to learn and grow from your experience, you must be objective and logical in your assessment, rather than making rash and unsubstantiated assumptions.

Firstly, you need to reflect on your own performance to establish any possible areas for improvement. You can then make adjustments as necessary and shift your focus to the next opportunity.

Firstly, you need to reflect on your own performance to establish any possible areas for improvement. In this assessment, you could ask:

Did I dress appropriately?
How did I sound?
Did I arrive on time?
Did I remember to smile?
Did I appear confident and relaxed?
Could my answers have been improved?
Did I maintain appropriate eye contact?
Did I establish rapport with the recruiter?

If this assessment identifies any weaknesses, you can make adjustments as necessary and shift your focus to the next opportunity.

Accept

Sometimes factors exist that are beyond your control and the unfortunate outcome may not have been directly influenced by your performance at all. In this instance, all you can do is accept the outcome and shift your focus to the next opportunity.

Be positive

Whatever the reason for rejection, it is important to treat each setback as a learning experience. So, don't become obsessive or overly critical, keep an open mind and be open to change if necessary. By handling the setback in this way, you will move forward and succeed much more quickly.

I would love

TO HEAR FROM YOU

If you have enjoyed reading this guide and have found it useful, I would love to hear from you, so please consider leaving your feedback.

www.CabinCrew.Guide

Where dreams are made

Facebook

Want to learn more?

CHECK OUT THE BESTSELLING BOOK

The Cabin Crew Interview
Made Easy

www.CabinCrew.Guide

Where dreams are made